Energy Healing Made Simple

Om Kitty's 8 Day Chakra Activation Journey

(Bonus: Learn To Banish Your Doubts About 'Woo-Woo' and Stop Worrying What Others Think)

The OM Kitty Series – Book 1
Sarah Saint-Laurent

Energy Healing Made Simple Om Kitty's 8 Day Chakra Activation Journey

Copyright © 2016 Sarah Saint-Laurent. All Rights Reserved.

This book or any portion thereof may not be reproduced or used in any manner whatsoever without the express written permission of the author except for the use of brief quotations in a book review.

Disclaimer: The information provided herein is for educational and informational purposes only and solely as a self-help tool for your own use. Always seek the advice of your own Medical Provider and/or Mental Health Provider regarding any questions or concerns you have about your specific health or any medications, herbs or supplements you are currently taking and before implementing any recommendations or suggestions from any outside source. Do not disregard medical advice or delay seeking medical advice if necessary. This book is not intended as a substitute for the medical advice of physicians. Do not start or stop taking any medications without speaking to your own Medical Provider or Mental Health Provider. If you have or suspect that you have a medical or mental health problem, contact your own Medical Provider or Mental Health Provider promptly.

Although the author and publisher have made every effort to ensure that the information in this book was correct at press time, the author and publisher do not assume and hereby disclaim any liability to any party for any loss, damage, or disruption caused by errors or omissions, whether such errors or omissions result from negligence, accident, or any other cause.

Cover design by: Stellaris
Chakra art design: Sarah Saint-Laurent
Editing by: Vicki Lowry
Printed in the United States of America

Advance Praise for *OM Kitty* – Reader's Reviews

The most divine path is often the simplest one. If you're curious about chakras and long to feel good, this is the fabulously feline CliffsNotes of energy healing. Om Kitty is so wise! I can't wait to play with her week of energy healing.

— Sarah Seidelmann M.D. of followyourfeelgood.com and author of *What the Walrus Knows: An Eccentric's Field Guide to Working with Beastie Energies*

I have read a lot of books, articles and guides on energy and chakra healing, spiritual growth, stress management, and the like, and I find OM Kitty to be the easiest, most accessible, most delightful energy healing guide out there. OM Kitty speaks with such delight, earnestness, simplicity, compassion, conciseness and clarity, I couldn't put it down and will be recommending this highly to friends, colleagues, family, and clients - especially those who are skeptical of energy healing or claim they don't have time. OM Kitty practically sits on your lap and purrs and smiles and heals just with her presence and beautiful, loving, encouraging words. Congratulations on putting your original medicine and magic in the world.

—Lauren Oujiri, M.A. Martha Beck Certified Life Coach, Writer, Speaker, Reiki Master, <u>Lauren Oujiri Coaching</u>

I have always been a "spiritual" woman, but was raised conservatively and rarely ventured outside my standard comfort zone as I walked my spiritual journey. As a part of my spiritual growth last year, I began exploring other practices such as meditation, reiki and other alternative healing methods. While I've fallen in love with these alternative spiritual growth and self-help practices, how I wish I could have had Om Kitty as my guide while I was experiencing my awakening!

Om Kitty is soul-filled, wise and sophisticated all at the same time. As a certified Life Coach, a healer, a teacher and reiki master, I plan on sharing Om Kitty with many of my clients (and friends as well) who are intrigued by energy healing and spirituality but may be inhibited by being too "woo-woo" or judged by others.

Thank you, Om Kitty!

—Julie E. Cline, Certified Life Coach, Reiki Master & Guide
www.myonehappylife.com

Om Kitty is a funny, brilliant, modern-day sage whose wit and wisdom spans the ages. Sarah Saint Laurent *shares ancient wisdom and fundamental truths of how to heal ourselves and our busy lives through the voice of a cat whose company is as irresistible and comfortable as a best friend. It is not easy to make the secrets of the universe available to the every day person, but Om Kitty manages to do it! And she makes us smile the whole time!*

— Beth Gager, Author of A <u>Rooted Mind - Saying Yes To Beauty, Wellness And Deeply-Rooted Mental Health</u> and Certified Life Coach.

OM Kitty is a delightfully modern-day character who is witty and wise in sharing truths in how to heal. Using Energy Healing techniques, we can learn to heal our busy, frenetic lives simply and easily by listening to Om Kitty's wise advice and ancient guidance. She covers the Chakra Systems, abundant living, and energy frequency just to name a few things. Her guidance is easy to use and delightful to absorb; and it's fun!

Pamme Mickelson – Non-Profit Executive Director, Santa Barbara California

This book is a cute and funny way to send out a message to those who need to start on the path to exploring the wise truths of how to heal and save ourselves. We are given a bit of humor to taste these new treats by the em-

ployment of a sweet kitty and her secrets for living a happier and more fulfilled life. Using some simple tools like energy healing, working to heal the chakras and reiki as well as other ancient wisdoms to start a novice on their path is hard to accomplish, but this kitty manages to do it in a wonderful way. A delightful way to introduce these subjects. I am looking forward to more of this type of work from this author.

— Karen Wheeler, Florida

Om Kitty is my first introduction into this kind of energy work. Before reading, I had no idea how to do chakra healing. Om Kitty explains it all in easy to understand language and walks you through simple steps for self-healing. I love how fun she makes it and takes the judgment away for all to accept these ideas. i have practiced these processes since reading this book and it works! I have felt lighter, more energetic, happier and healthier! Thank you, OM Kitty!

— Kristen Hummell – Healthy Living Strategist, Whidbey Island WA

I speak and write on the Hero's Journey that awaits each of us if we are willing to go for it. OM Kitty has embraced

her own Hero's Journey and took her life and the lives of other's who join her, to an entirely new level. Before reading **Energy Healing Made Simple – OM Kitty's 8 Day Chakra Activation Journey**, I had little personal knowledge of energy work and how important it is. Om Kitty has shared a unique, fun and simple way of understanding Energy Healing techniques, the Chakra Systems, and how my own frequency determines my happiness level. I really loved this book. It's fun, easy to read and with its practical tools and exercises, you can use it as a daily journal. So if you want to bring light in your life, come with me and follow Om Kitty.

— Emmanuelle Guerrin, Paris, France, Certified Life Coach - specializing in Hero's Journey work. www.emlifecoach.com

OM Kitty's 8 Day Chakra Activation Journey is a great way to get your feet wet with energy healing and chakras. This is a nice way to step lightly into a path of spirituality. OM Kitty's occasional words of feline wisdom are timely and fun loving, making my mind-body healing path just a little bit easier.

— Melisa Sharpe, www.melcoaching.com

I loved reading Om Kitty! What I love about it is it is easy to connect to and provides short practices that I can

use right now (and with my life, that is a good thing)! Sarah Saint Laurent shares her insight and truths of how to heal ourselves and OM kitty is just the right vehicle to give us this information. There was so much provided on the Chakra System and energy, as well as how to live from abundance. I love this book and will keep coming back to it over and over again!

— Rebecca Shisler Marshal, coach and yogini, www.CenteredYou.com

Sarah Saint-Laurent has written a simple and accessible guide to working with one's chakras with this first book in her series. She lays out an easy-to-follow series of steps that allow readers of all levels of interest to cleanse their energetic systems. What I enjoyed most about the book is the set of intentions she offers and suggests before doing this work. This stating of intentions reminded me somehow of magical spells, and I think that somehow, that's where the real magic in living comes from, in the setting and stating of our deepest intentions, and I'm grateful to her for reminding me of that. I look forward to seeing how the rest of the series progresses!

— Yuichi Handa, California

*Note to Reader-

I purposefully use the term 'woo-woo' a lot in this book to attract the attention of readers who might grapple with a tug of war between their innate curiosity toward deeper connection and spirituality and their mind's limiting belief that this is 'weird.' In general, 'woo-woo' has come to mean a belief or attraction to things that cannot be explained scientifically or are 'unprovable.' Dr. Deepak Chopra is quoted as saying: "...the term, "woo woo" is a derogatory reference to almost any form of unconventional thinking, aimed by professional skeptics who are self-appointed vigilantes dedicated to the suppression of curiosity." (Huffington Post 3/18/2010)

If you were to exchange the term 'woo-woo' with more positive words or phrases such as, enlightenment, connection, authentic, ancient wisdom traditions, quantum physics, sensory threshold, leading edge you would find you no longer are at war with yourself and are free to follow your natural inclination towards seeking truth.

In addition to accessing the power of energy healing, this book will assist you in letting go of your fear of embracing 'woo-woo.'

Dearest One ~ Hello and welcome.

"Change me Divine Beloved into one who knows that You alone are my Source. Let me trust that You fling open every door at the right time. Free me from the illusion of rejection, competition, and scarcity.

Fill me with confidence and faith, knowing I never have to beg, just gratefully receive."

— Tosha Silver, Change Me Prayers: The Hidden Power of Spiritual Surrender

Dear reader, as a token of my affection, please copy this link into your browser to receive The OM Kitty Kit-and-Caboodles Freebie Package. A special gift consisting of additional tools to help you on your journey. You can download for free now or later here:

http://wp.me/P5D95B-lA

Enjoy!

For S and G – of course!

And for the Wayfinders

A note of gratitude:

I have profound gratitude for the many people who assisted me in bringing this first book in The OM Kitty Book Series this far. Without the support of my very dear friends and associates this task would never have been so smooth. I am eternally grateful, especially to my advance readers. You have my heart.

Table of Contents

Part One

The *Why* Of Energy Healing..1

Finding Your Authentic Self Through Energy Healing......3

When I Thought It Was All Mumbo-Jumbo....................7

When Fear Of Rejection Takes Hold..................................9

Forget What You Think You Know..................................11

Letting Go Of Limiting Rules..13

When The 'Woo-Woo' Rings True Instead Of Sounds Weird..15

Bridging The Physical And Spiritual Aspects....................19

Finding A Key To A Treasure Chest..................................21

Part Two
The *How* Of Energy Healing..25

What Is Energy Healing?..27

Why Energy Healing Is A Game Changer........................31

The Importance Of Letting Go Of Story..........................33

A Note On Emotional Release..35

Additional Suggestions And Tools...37

Introduction To The Chakra System 43

Part Three
Healing And Clearing Your Energy Centers
The 8 Day Journey..67

Day 1 Bringing In The Light 69

Day 2 The Root Chakra...81

Day 3 The Sacral Chakra..85

Day 4 The Solar Plexus Chakra...89

Day 5 Heart Chakra...93

Day 6 Throat Chakra...97

Day 7 3rd Eye Chakra...101

Day 8 Crown Chakra..105

The Next Step 109

A Note Of Gratitude 111

About The Author 113

Part One
The *Why* of Energy Healing

Finding your Authentic Self through Energy Healing...

Do you secretly crave a life that embraces a different level of clarity and peace through:

- Profound spiritual practices,
- Effortless abundance,
- Magical manifestation,
- And deep, rejuvenating healing?

But at the same time struggle with fear-based thoughts that these things are:

- for 'those other people,'
- those 'woo-woo' people,
- and not you?

If so, congratulations, you've found the right book. Energy Healing is the most expedient path to living a life of abundance and well-being and can be learned and practiced by anyone at any time, including you. You just need to decide that your health and happiness are more important than the opinions of others.

This book was written specifically for those who want to stretch and lean into a deeper connection with 'The Divine Love' but wonder about things like:

- 'Is it really OK to try this? Or have I lost my mind?'
- 'What will my spouse... Parents... Boss... think? OMG, what will my friends say?'
- 'Does this put me in the 'bad' column?' 'Am I harming my soul? My church doesn't like this woo-woo stuff.'
- 'I'm a professional. I'm educated. This is too looney. People will think I've gone mad!'
- 'Do you have to be a vegan and member of PETA and wear long flowing caftans to do this or can 'regular' folks do this too?'

This book is designed to give you a simple, easy to follow 8 Day Journey into Energy Healing and Chakra Activation and is packed full of insights and tools to help you understand this amazing method for healing yourself at the deepest level and building the momentum necessary to live the life of your dreams. Although purposefully designed for beginners and those wanting to tip-toe into something new and exciting, this journey will benefit anyone seeking a new level of well-being and freedom.

In addition to being an introduction to the Chakra System, this book also provides bonus tools to understand how your body works as your own personal GPS and how to be aware of what your physical body is telling you so that you can better hear the inner voice of your Higher Self singing out, asking you to return home, to your soul's calling.

When I thought it was all mumbo-jumbo...

Once, in a different cat life, I thought Energy Healing and all the other spiritual, mystical, metaphysical 'mumbo jumbo' were a myth or at best a hoax and something to be *avoided*. I clung to a torturous story that anything new and different wasn't for me. Anything 'strange and out-there' was for those 'weird' people, those 'new-agers,' not a nice, normal little kitten like me. Does this sound familiar?

You see, I was once exactly where you are. In my first cat life, I secretly yearned to be free of my self-imposed shackles that kept me small and deeply rooted in my pain. I secretly wanted to explore spiritual growth and to quest after my soul's calling. Deep inside I could sense my life could be more joyful, free and easy. But I was ruled by fear-based thoughts and was afraid I would disappoint others. So I never leaped into my true happiness and instead I shrank into a small ball of fur and smoothed my whiskers back into place and went about living my false existence.

I wore a well-crafted mask of satisfaction to disguise my internal dissatisfaction, unhappiness, and complacency. In fact, I was secretly disgruntled almost all the time but hid it well from any prying eyes. I was too afraid to let anyone know I desperately wanted to step outside my well-structured box of mediocrity and hidden unhappiness. My façade was impeccable.

Yet still, I knew there had to be more. I could feel a tugging at my heart and an excited stirring of my mind whenever life caused me to brush up on intriguing new concepts and ideas that spoke to my Higher-Self. However, the more I thought about these concepts and ideas the greater my discomfort and fear became. So I shrank even smaller.

When fear of rejection takes hold...

Deep inside, my *heart* said yes to new and daring ways of accessing a stronger connection to God, the Universe, the angel realm, or simply consciousness at a different level. My *body* wanted to leap with wild abandon toward exploring beguiling new experiences such as mysticism, mind-body centeredness, and guided visualization. I wanted to deliberately create a new, fulfilled life, unfurling my tail and unleashing my claws and to bravely step away from my well-rehearsed script of 'acceptability at all cost.'

But my *mind* said absolutely not. I was afraid of change. I was paralyzed with fear; fear of rejection by my faith community, fear of abandonment by my friends and loved ones, fear of being considered silly, strange or even bonkers. I did not possess the stamina or fortitude to follow my soul's desire. I handed my personal power over to others, clinging to the perception that their views and opinions were more valid than my own. I lived in a quagmire of approval dependency. And so my first life was spent trudging through the trenches of being acceptable, fitting in and living in self-inflicted mediocrity. Then I died.

You see, that is what happens when you do not seek your bliss. You *exist* but you don't truly live, and then you die. But that doesn't have to be your story. Energy healing has become my secret catalyst to repair, rejuvenation, clarity and above all peace and joy.

If you can, for just a moment, let go of viewing yourself as a run-of-the-mill ordinary, unhappy and stuck-in-a-rut person and instead think of yourself as a Super-Hero in your own epic life adventure. As a Super-Hero, you are now ready to engage and transport yourself to the level of living you are meant to have, and Energy Healing will be your super-power.

Energy Healing is not just for 'those other people,' it is for you, right here and right now. How do I know? Because I once was just like you and I lived with these same fears. Unlike me, you probably aren't a cat with 9 lives. You likely have this one life and it needs to be your One True Life. The good news is that healing your energy system is the fastest and simplest path to allow and usher in abundant well-being, whether it is emotional, physical, spiritual or even financial.

Forget what you think you know...

You may be wondering 'how do I make this leap of faith and explore energy healing and my soul's calling?' You might be biting your lip while thinking 'others might question my sanity!' To make this leap you need to forget every limiting concept you've been taught by your parents, grandparents, schools and society. This is the only way to transform your *existence* into your One True Life.

You must take what you have been *told* is true and turn it upside down. Then you need to turn it backward and finally turn it inside out. Stop doubting yourself and believing other people know what is right for you. Trust yourself. Let go of the shackles that stop you from exploring your truth and allow what you have been told to slip away and instead allow what you *know* to be true be your guidance system. Now you will have something to work with. But *how* you might ask?

You begin by recalling who you really are. When you arrived here in your physical form you knew you were intrinsically connected to The One Great Love. The problem is most of us forget this fact very early on. You must recall who you really are and how important your life really is.

Then, you choose to forget the rules and the 'shoulds' that have been regurgitated for thousands of years that cause you to live a small fear-based life. These rules and 'shoulds' are not based in reality. They are simply stories that have been engineered by the minds of humans and propagated throughout history on a mass conscious level. These rules may only exist in the mind but we believe them and we buy into them to our detriment. You know your truth because it lives inside you and is just waiting for you to allow it to come forth.

Letting go of limiting Rules...

I refer to these structured mind-based rules as 'crules' because they are insidious and cruel, not only to ourselves but to society as a whole. 'Crules' are non-reality based rules formed in the fleeting imagination of someone else. We have even come to understand these 'crules' as 'long-standing truths' and 'moral obligations.' But they are neither of these things.

Think about this short list of 'cruels,' stories we have been told our whole life and believe to hold weight and then decide if they are irrefutably true:

- Taking care of yourself first is selfish.
- Money equals success.
- You should have a college degree.
- Work requires effort.
- No pain – No gain.

- You should marry.
- You should have children.
- You should own a home.
- You should dress your age.
- You must have credit.
- Being alone is lonely.
- Working hard and fast is the best path to achievement.
- Pursuing your bliss is a pipedream.
- Being sensitive or an introvert is negative.
- Being a 'go-getter' or an extrovert is a positive.
- Naps are for lazy people.
- Having your head in the clouds is a bad idea.
- Blood is thicker than water.
- You owe your family allegiance.
- Failure is not an option.
- Time is money.

When the 'woo-woo' rings true instead of sounds weird...

Perhaps you have begun to question this traditional line of thinking, these dogmas, and myths that have shaped your own personal life. You are beginning to sense that you can be happier and more fulfilled by shifting your perspective. You glimpse that turning your thoughts around provides freedom and with this freedom you feel empowered to seek out your true purpose and follow your bliss.

You finally feel OK to pursue things that before now may have seemed too strange or 'woo-woo.' You feel your intuition ignited, you feel lighter and boundless instead of heavy and burdened. You are ready to dive in deep and unlock your potential and heal any and all pain.

Lucky for me I am a cat. I have more than one life so it was OK that my first life was traumatic, anxiety-ridden, painful and devoid of peace. Starting with my second iteration here things were different. I no longer possessed the fear I knew during my first life. I no longer clung to those limiting thoughts and behaviors that formerly kept my life so limited. When I re-emerged I was aligned with my deep knowing, my magic, and my ancient connection to the Source of all things, which I prefer to call God or Spirit, but feel free to insert whatever term you resonate with.

I was able to recall my soul-spark, my true essence, my divine purpose. My quest for spiritual fulfillment knew no barriers and I was free of any shackle or bindings which kept me small and feeling insignificant and trapped. I knew who and what I truly was, namely pure, positive energy connected at all times to a benevolent, generous source of pure love and awareness. I was free to embrace the deep stirring of my soul and so I experimented with everything spiritual.

Throughout my various incarnations, I have spent countless hour's fine-tuning my quest for joy. With every lifetime, I have acquired more tools, more inspiration from learned mentors, more clarity, and more freedom. I've absorbed works on the language of God, on ancient wisdom traditions, sacred contracts, the divine feminine, the wild-woman archetype and conscious awareness and mysticism to name just a few. Now I share what I have learned with my readers in an effort to help launch you on your right path.

If this resonates with you and you don't want to waste another minute of your precious life then I applaud you and offer my assistance. This 8-Day journey is intended as a short and basic introduction into energy healing. Yet it is a powerful and efficient means to start your path of deeper understanding and connection with your higher self.

It is time for you to remember who you are and why you came here in the first place. We came here to recall our connection and establish a sense or feeling of homecoming here on earth. We came here to experience inspiration, to understand and allow guidance and enjoy and explore new experiences with others. We came here to do all of this through joy. The purpose of living is found in joy. The result of joyful living is freedom. But joy and freedom can only come from choosing to engineer your own self-care and self-healing. Living your true, authentic self is allowing freedom to be born and to grow and to define your essential self. Through this, you may then engineer your own bliss. You must *choose* to purposefully engineer your own joy and freedom and the simplest method is through energy healing.

Know that Spirit loves you for simply being here now. You cannot create your bliss from outside Spirit only from within Spirit. Enjoy and embrace this dive into bliss and allow Spirit to work through you.

Bridging the physical and spiritual aspects...

Our energy system is the bridge between our anatomical structure (our physical body) and our conscious awareness (our soul.) Healing energy blocks and moving and releasing trapped toxicity from our energy systems, also known as our Chakra system, is the cornerstone of building a well-rooted life filled with joy, abundance, and clarity.

If you have lost your joy, you will regain it through energy healing. Fear of stepping into unknown territories is a roadblock to joy. If deepening your understanding of source energy and your relationship with the One Great Love sounds true in your heart, let nothing cause an obstacle. When you feel it, this calling, it is like a clamoring, gonging cymbal of recognition. Let all perceptions by others fall to the wayside. Allow Energy Healing, like a golden thread that pulls you homeward, to be your connection.

Finding a Key to a treasure chest...

Something very important came from all of the pain, suffering and broken-heartedness I endured in my first cat life. I came to understand that I must know what I *don't* want in order to know what I *do* want. That is an essential key to pursuing your One True Life. Is it painful and uncomfortable? Yes. And it is revealing and inspiring as well.

Energy healing gave me the keys to a magical treasure chest. In this treasure trove, I keep my vast wealth, which includes my courage, clarity, relief, intuition, and peace. With these stores of wealth, I am aligned with my deepest resonance and I am free to discern what I truly want and that which no longer serves me. Along the way, I learned many important things about myself and I'll share just a few.

- Seeking the approval of others is useless. Let go of this myth immediately.

- I no longer accept the concept of Duality, which is the dwelling place of judgment and suffering. I learned no one way is right.

- I can be spiritually conscious on my own terms. I am not required to adhere to anyone's opinions or ways in order to live my fullest expression of my Higher Self.

- I rescued myself by letting go of my need to rescue others.

- I am not God so I no longer try to control everyone else's universe.

- I don't particularly like wheat grass juice.

- I enjoy keeping my energy healing and meditation short and focused. If you are like me, you might not have time to sit on a meditation cushion for 1-2 hours a day. 15 minutes is sufficient for me and very doable.

- I love wearing my tiara with the sassy Om Symbol in the center no matter how many other people might find it too flashy.

- I love walking and speaking in my own personal truth. When I am authentic, I have greater momentum allowing me to easily follow my path of least resistance.

- I don't resonate with this new, popular mantra of being a 'Bad-Ass.' That goes for 'bad-assery' and 'Epic F*&%ing Bad-Ass' too. I don't want to be a bad anything, let alone an ass. My persona is one of sophisticated caring. I don't ever want to be considered a 'Bad-Ass.' And if you don't like the word "sophisticated", then I bless you anyway.

- I naturally expect to be treated with respect, love and nurturing. Therefore, I receive it in copious forms and amounts. My Inner Being stands in resonance with all that I truly am and by knowing this I allow abundance to flow. Energy Healing assists with knowing your own Inner Being intimately.

- Energy Healing helped me deepen my understanding of deep spirituality which did not erase my original faith in my creator but instead strengthened it.

- I love finding magic in the smallest things and watch as my path unfolds as the universe ushers in constant magical moments.

- I love embracing my preferences. I may be a healer, mender and intuitive kitten but I also love a really good black bag, ice-cold cream in a fine china saucer and a super plush blanket. I cannot do without excellent milk chocolate with whole almonds (preferably Swiss.) Cashmere scarves are a must.

- I love being serene and contemplative, nurturing and compassionate. Yet I also love being feisty, fierce, confident and irreverent.

- I love long naps in the sun and really good books to read.

- I love being silent and I love to talk.

That's enough about me. Let's start healing some energy in a really fun and simple way. I am honored to be your guide on this eight-day journey to simple energy healing. I welcome you to a new life, new joy, new healing, and new abundance.

Part Two
The *How* of Energy Healing

What is Energy Healing?

Energy is the mechanism that constructs the universe, the cosmos, our homes, our refrigerators, daffodils, lemurs, cargo ships and us. Everything is made of energy. Each and every one of us is an energetic being and at the atomic level, all things are a constellation of energy waves that vibrate at certain frequencies.

We are also inextricably attached to that which created this universe; the source of all that is or ever was or will be. This source, called Spirit or Consciousness or God is pure awareness and pure love and our connection, moving through and with this source, is pure positive energy. The part of ourselves we are unable to physically see is the greater, larger and truer version of ourselves. The merest intrinsic attribute of our truest self is pure, positive energy and this we may call our soul or Higher Self. Our soul is the energetic expression of 'The Great One Love,' now and forever and it is boundless, joyful and blissful.

However, we all will have experienced pain and loss at some time in our lives. This pain and suffering have a purpose and it is called contrast. For without contrast, we would not have joy. That may sound counterintuitive but it is true.

Without experiencing that which you do not want, you would be helpless to know definitively, what you do want. The Swiss psychoanalyst Carl G. Jung said: "The word 'happiness' would lose its meaning if it were not balanced by sadness." What this is intended to point to is it is impossible to know one without knowing the other. Your soul directs you to all joyful things that feel good. When you feel otherwise, you are not aligned with your Higher Self. The discomfort now becomes a beacon of light pointing you back home. Energy Healing is the most expedient means to locate and clear this discomfort and align with your true nature.

If you are having trouble with this concept, do not simply throw it away. Think about it. Without the 'one terrible, horrible, really awful, creepy, bad thing happening; that icky, ugly thing that made you feel so broken, or anxious or enraged, betrayed, or a myriad of other negative emotions, without it having happened, how could you possibly know that you never under any circumstance want that back in your life?

You couldn't. Aren't you better off knowing that you never want to experience that again? If you say yes, then you are on your way to freedom. Freedom is born through clarity.

Through pain and loss, we, as small children learned to experience emotional upheaval and developed creative and curious coping mechanisms, most being completely unsuitable for thriving adults.

Fear of Rejection...

Fear is the basis for all dysfunction. We fear many things but universally what we fear the most is rejection. In fact, I believe rejection is the base fear of everything. Our ability to learn to survive and cope with emotional pain and fear was hardwired into our brains by at a very young age. The problem is we are left to grow up with defense mechanisms and coping skills of unskilled toddlers.

We learned to either run, fight or ingratiate our way out of sticky situations. The result is a gooey mess of pent up negative energy. This is hopeless. When fear is evident, alive and stuck in our energetic system, our beautiful Chakras becomes blocked.

As adults, we may have learned to eliminate fear-based limiting thoughts through inquiry. We can dissolve limiting thoughts by seeing their invalidity and we can turn these thoughts around to more purposeful and truer thoughts.

But then what? We have let go of a nagging, limiting fear-based thought. We feel good about that and we enjoy our new freedom in understanding a different view, a better truth or belief. That is a wonderful beginning. However, are we healed?

Why Energy Healing is a Game Changer...

In my first cat life, I heard the call to explore energy healing. However, I chose to ignore it. I was exceedingly reluctant to step into this area. I simply could not wrap my head around the concept of an 'energetic system' that governed not only my physical body but my spiritual essence and wellbeing. I was entrenched in my stubbornness to discard the concept of 'energy' out of fear of disapproval by others. Although my heart and soul yearned for clarity and deep healing, my mind would not allow me to take a leap of faith.

It was not until my second cat life that I entertained the concept of energy healing in any committed way. I began to do my research. Over the course of a few years, I became what you might consider an arm-chair quantum physics geek. The science behind the 'energy' claims was not only authoritative, it was impossible to argue against. So now my mind was square with my heart.

At the atomic level, we are quivering strings of pure, cosmic energy and that is where any and all healing needs to occur. If both "Dis-ease" and "Disease" are caused by our pervasive fear-based thoughts, then it stands to reason that complete healing requires the clearing of this fear at the most basic level, the cellular level, through deep energy healing and activation.

The seven primary Chakras are energetic centers running along the spine acting as connectors between our conscious and physiological systems. They govern the core emotional and physical functions of our Being. These energy centers hold on to the negative energy caused by fear based thoughts even after the thought has been dissolved. That is why complete healing requires energy clearing, thereby removing the blocked or traumatic energy at the cellular level. In my own personal experience, I can say I only realized pure, complete healing when I allowed myself to bravely dive into the ancient and well-established practice of energy healing.

Once you have mastered your energy vibration through clearing and releasing, you will be more intuitive and you will be more present. You will begin to be aware of people, places, and situations at a more acute level. This will make it easy for you to allow the unseen forces of heaven and the universe usher in abundance, clarity, joy, and bliss.

The Importance of Letting Go of Story...

As you make this healing journey you may notice that 'thoughts' or 'things' or even just good old 'Crap' comes up. You may find you forget to make time to heal; you found yourself short on time and couldn't fit it in yesterday and maybe even tomorrow. You may also find while you are engaged in the 8-day healing journey you find it difficult to focus or sit still. You may worry that you are not doing it right.

Always remember to be kind to yourself, now and forever. I believe you can never really get it wrong and you can never really get it perfectly right. There is no such thing as perfection. Perfection is simply a mental construct designed to keep people in a never ending circle of sabotage. Let go of the stories you tell yourself about 'never having enough time, 'I'm not doing this right' and 'I'm not able to focus.'

Simply take the time, commit yourself to 'allowing' this precious time for yourself. Make yourself a priority and choose to give yourself a break. Let go of the need to judge yourself during this process. Let go of the story you tell yourself, the one that limits you.

Approach this journey with the intention to be open to healing. Allow your mind and heart to resonate with the truth shared by both your bodily sensations and the inner voice of wisdom. Allow yourself freedom from worrying about 'doing it right.' Keep thoughts of 'failing' from entering your awareness. Simply chose to begin with this 8 Day Journey. You will then likely find the right and best way for you to reap the benefits from energy healing, making it a lifelong part of your life's journey.

A Note on Emotional Release...

The Purpose of Energy Healing is to release toxic residue and blockages contained within the Chakra or Energy System. You can think of the Chakra System as a database. A full description of the 7 Chakras is described below. However, I want to point out here that as in all healing, whether a scraped knee or a serious wound, it is likely you will feel some discomfort or even a lot of discomfort. Please understand you are not alone. This is perfectly normal and it is also necessary. I have gone through this process and I continue to go through this process whenever I am ready to heal at a deeper level. Do not be afraid of discomfort. Understand it is temporary and will pass.

When I began healing my own energy, I could recall trauma from my first cat-life. This coupled with newly experienced pain caused some doubt. There were times I was absolutely afraid. I was afraid that if I opened up my closed box of pain experienced in my first life along with milder forms of hurt experienced in my current life, I might fall down and never get back up off the floor. The thought of possibly sinking into depression and that ugly dark blanket of despair was constantly in the back of my mind. I was assured by my own energy healing mentor that this is normal and it is simply a thought I was having. It was not based in reality. Think of this time as 'fleeting' because it is not permanent.

If you have this kind of thought, please know that you will get up off the floor. In fact, what you might find, like I did, is that you don't fall on the floor at all. I found that the 'thinking' I had over the possibility of depression and falling down on the floor was simply me escalating my fear. In a nutshell, it didn't happen. Did I have emotional discomfort? Absolutely. But it was completely manageable. It was nothing like how my mind was imagining it would be. And once I experienced the release through the discomfort, that particular area of pain ceased to exist.

**Important note: Please my dearest one, if you are in the deep throes of depression or are dealing with any clinical mental diagnosis, please honor yourself and continue seeing your clinical therapist or medical professional. If this is you and you do not currently have a medical professional please do seek out professional help at your earliest opportunity.

Additional Suggestions and Tools

Energy Healing is so simple, it requires nothing other than being present with your mind, soul and body. However, before I begin the introduction to the Chakra System I would like to share with you some of my favorite tools and a few friendly suggestions that you may enjoy incorporating into your practice.

Keeping a Healing or Energy-Work Journal

Use a journal to jot down thoughts, emotions, questions, doodles, some sacred geometry sketch, a poem that materialized out of nowhere, song lyrics, a smoothie recipe, a curious thought that popped up and, as well, to chart your progress as you move through this eight-day journey. If you end up keeping a journal you will be amazed at your success and achievements when you reflect back on the recorded insights, messages, stirrings, 'Aha-moments' and growth contained in your writings.

If you find yourself dreaming more during the Energy Healing Journey, this is perfectly normal. Your mind is in a relaxed place while you sleep and your Soul is communicating with you. Your energy healing journal is the perfect place to write down your dreams, even a short dream snippet. You can then take this dream message into your energy healing to manifest insight and direction.

Create a Divine Space

There is a purpose in having a Divine Space. Hopefully, you can find a space that will be yours alone. Clear the space of all unnecessary objects. Clutter causes chaos to exist in our minds. We feel the presence of unwanted, unnecessary or disorganized belongings and it affects our subconsciousness. It is good to 'Clear the Plate' when beginning a chakra healing or balancing journey. When you designate a space to enjoy your daily journey, clear and declutter it.

Make this a Divine Space, one of peace, calm and tranquility. If possible, add loveliness to it by bringing in a fresh flower bud in a small vase, and having a warm, cozy wrap or blanket available to cuddle up in. Ventilate your space out by opening windows and consider burning white sage, known as "smudging" to clear the space.

As you sit and become accustomed to your divine space, you may very well find you 'need' to declutter many other areas of your life. Healing is like that. It can permeate into every area of our life. By cleansing your personal spaces on a regular basis, you can create a more peaceful environment and peaceful life.

Create a Ritual

Nothing is better than creating a beautiful ritual in which to heal. Think of this as creating an exotic gift for yourself, a silent, special time in which you do the same thing every day.

Here are some ideas:

- Awaken at the same time every day and begin your journey. Before getting out of bed bring 5 thoughts of gratitude to mind. Bless yourself and others.

- Create a Daily Mantra for the Day and repeat it 5 times before beginning your daily journey. An example might be 'Today I am open to magic and beauty happening as I effortlessly move through my day.'

- Keep fresh flowers in your Divine Space.

- Cleanse your hands and face and apply essential lavender oil to your wrists and pressure points of the face.

- Sit in the same place every day wrapped in a beautiful, soft shawl.

- Ring a bell or small gong.

- Write a small note setting out your intention for healing that day.

Helpful Tools

This list is intended only to be a suggestion and it is not exhaustive. Consider the suggestions and feel how they resonate inside your body. If it 'feels' good, consider implementing the tool in your healing journey.

Music: No need to invest in music when there are lovely meditation music tracks available on YouTube. I sometimes choose to use Shamanic drumming music during intense healing sessions. Another suggestion is to use no music and instead, find a tract of crashing waves or gentle rainfall, or forest animal sounds.

Crystals: The use of crystals and precious stones is an ancient practice used in healing. You can order a simple crystal kit for energy healing from the internet. Most people choosing to use crystals place the crystal directly upon the body part corresponding with the Chakra System being healed or activated.

Incense: I love incense and I even take it with me when traveling. The use of incense is a common practice in most world spiritual practices. It is said that the smoke rising from the burning incense is a metaphor for our prayers and intentions drifting upward to heaven.

The use of incense is thought to relieve stress. Incense like aromatherapy activates one of our five senses, the sense of smell. This can assist us with focus and concentration. I am fond of sandalwood and patchouli. But you may find you prefer a lighter scent.

Introduction to the Chakra System

The word Chakra in Sanskrit translates to 'Wheel.' Energy Center and Chakra are interchangeable and there are 7 primary energetic centers. Below I make it easy for you to know the symbol, color, and sound of each Chakra. Here is what the basic Chakra system looks like moving from Crown to Root. To activate the healing as we work through the book, consider visualizing the Energy Center spinning clockwise as you silently repeat the sound of the Chakra.

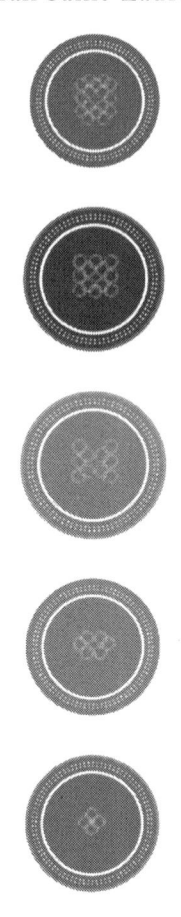

The 7 Chakras are as follows:

The 1st Energy Center: <u>The Root Chakra is the Muladhara</u> – (The Foundation) and is broken down into two Sanskrit words: Mula meaning "root" and Adhara, which means, "support" or "base"

- Location: Base of spine.

- Symbol: 4 petal lotus

- Color: Bright Red

- Sanskrit Mantra - Sound: LAM (LUMmmmmmm)

This Base Chakra is the seat of our most basic human necessities, our basic primal and sustaining needs including, food, water, shelter and safety. This energy center governs our perceptions concerning security, stability, belonging, clan/tribe/family, faith, structures, and authority. Fears concerning shelter, finances, personal belongings, personal identity, and safety are rooted here.

Dysfunctional thought patterns involving Root Chakra: Failure, rejection, abandonment. Acute anxiety caused by uncertainty and depression often stem from blocked energy in our Root Chakra.

Truth Hint*: Do you have anxiety around basic core needs like money, shelter and safety? Maybe you don't even realize that you, in fact, have anxiety or discomfort from toxic build up in your root energy system. Perhaps you think it's everyone's experience to start hyperventilating or profusely sweating at the armpits when grocery shopping or paying bills even when knowing there is sufficient money for these necessities in the purse and checking account. If you are inexplicably queasy in even the most benign spending scenarios, and especially if you have more than enough money, then you have a blocked Muladhara.*

Did you know it is a pervasive universal fear of many women that they will become homeless one day? Females all over the world, regardless of ethnicity, social standing or location, share this fear. It is similar to a subliminal hypnosis. This shared fear, that one day they will be bag-ladies living under a bridge or down by the river in a tent with no running water, is a sub-conscious thought shared by countless women even though there is no basis for it in reality. Does it have to do with a preoccupation with material needs? No, it exists because these poor souls lacked the certainty of safety within their families of origin. This is not to say these women were all physically abused. There are many reasons one might feel unsafe in their family of origin. This lack of certainty of safety is alive and well with felines too and leaves many of us paralyzed with fear and living small lives.

When this is the case, our Root Chakra is severely blocked. This can be remedied through continuous energy release and healing. (There is also room for discussion as to how this is linked to the primordial loss of the divine feminine and loss of feminine power in the transition from an originally matriarchal / goddess society to a predominantly patriarchal / male God society but that is material reserved for another book coming soon.)

The 2nd Energy Center: <u>The Sacral Chakra is the Svadhisthana</u>, which can be translated in Sanskrit as "the dwelling place of the self." I like to refer to this Chakra as my 'space of creativity.'

- Location: Sits between the naval and the base of the spine.
- Symbol: 6 petal lotus
- Color: Bright Orange
- Sanskrit Mantra – Sound: VAM (VUMmmmmmm)

This Chakra is the wheelhouse of infinite creativity and birth as creativity reigns supreme in this center, birthplace to all forms of art and inspired endeavors. It is the domain of pleasure, desire, hopes, passion, sensuality, and sexuality. Home to both the masculine and feminine aspects co-existing in every being, the Sacral Chakra governs fertility, vitality and potency. An open and free flowing Svadhisthana allows intimate connection and when clear can work as a magnet of attraction.

Dysfunctional Thought Patterns involving Sacral Chakra: A lack mindset, overly concerned with physical appearance, lack of intimacy, inability to perceive beauty, inability to feel lovable. Addictions, whether through ingestion or by behavior, such as unnecessary spending of money, or over-work and exertion often stem from a block in our Sacral Chakra.

Truth Hint*: A blocked Sacral Chakra will hamper your connection with La Loba, the wild woman archetype. If you are unfamiliar with the extraordinary work by Dr. Clarissa Pinkola-Estaes, <u>Women Who Run With the Wolves</u> (Ballantine, 1992) I urge you to get a copy quickly! An important aspect of La Loba is the highly articulated intuition all females possess. This innate intuition will be depleted without the continuous use of your creative talents. What do you love to do? Dance, sing, write, paint, sculpt, sew, knit, garden? These are all creative endeavors which feed and hone your innate intuition. Maybe you love to cook or bake for your family. That is an expression of love and creativity from your Highest-Self. Honor yourself by honoring* *your creative calling. By doing so, you will activate the radiance of your Sacral Chakra and reap abundance and well-being.*

Regarding the two aspects, the female and male contained in the Svadhisthana of all living beings, each aspect is equally important. The female aspect is our deep connection to wisdom and our portal to our mystical intuition. This aspect is a life-giving force which nurtures and sustains. The male aspect is our connection to rational thinking, adaptability, and strength. Combined they promote harmony, desire, hope, and passion.

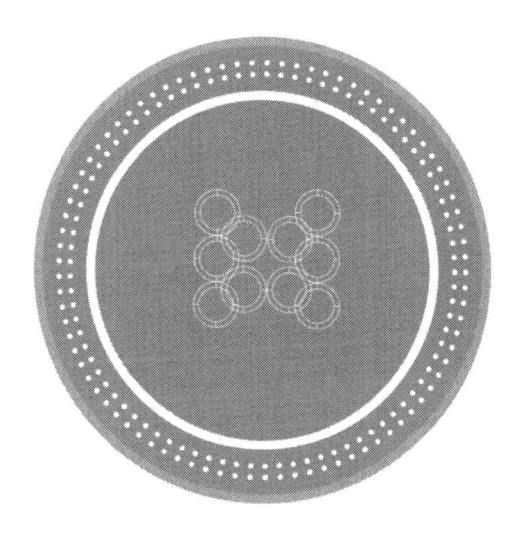

The 3rd Energy Center: <u>The Solar Plexus Chakra is the Manipura</u> translated in Sanskrit to mean Home of the lustrous Jewel and is the seat of your personal instinct and power.

- Location: Sits above your stomach and directly below the sternum or breastbone.

- Symbol: 10 petal lotus

- Color: Bright Yellow

- Sanskrit Mantra – Sound: RAM (RUMmmmmmmm)

This Chakra is the wheelhouse of interpersonal relationships, and governs gut instinct, free will, self-autonomy, self-worth, self-esteem and personal power. Sitting at the location of your digestive system, this 3rd Chakra relates to the ability to 'digest' your personal life and desires. A clear and free flowing Manipura allows for the effortless manifestation of intentions stemming from clarity through personal integrity – alignment with inner personal power.

Dysfunctional thought patterns involving Solar Plexus Chakra: Lack of Confidence, Lack of social acumen, lack of motivation and direction, inability to maintain healthy relationships with self or others. It will also indicate a lack of self-love, absence of invincibility, or powerlessness. When blocked energy is present, one will feel distrust, and lack of personal power. Powerlessness is a seriously limiting energy that can manifest in the perpetual victim mindset.

Truth Hint*: Are you a one-woman show? Do you avoid asking for and receiving help? Do you prefer to do everything yourself because you can do it faster and better without interference from others? This was one of my greatest limiting beliefs during my first cat life. My pervasive need to over-do for everyone and everything came from my inherent distrust. I did not <u>believe</u> that all would be well without my personal involvement. What this translates to is one very tired, unnecessarily stressed, perpetually grumpy kitten with a victim mindset and a bitter chip on her shoulder.*

Perfectionism and over-achieving are linked to a deep need for the approval of others. If this resonates with you, it may be that you only feel relevant when you are astoundingly needed by others (even when in reality you are not) and relied upon to the point of absurdity and quite possibly insanity. The one you really do not trust is yourself. That can be a hard pill to swallow. If this rings true at all with your soul, please pay special attention to the healing and release of toxic energy built up in your Solar Plexus Chakra.

The 4th Energy Center: <u>The Heart Chakra is the Anahatta.</u> This Sanskrit word means "unstruck" or "unhurt."

Anahatta is the power seat of Love. This 4th Chakra sits directly between the lower 3 Chakras and the Higher 3 Chakras and is the mediator of all healing. This energy center is the portal to divinity and the gateway to humanity.

- Location: Sits in the center of your chest directly behind your breastbone.
- Symbol: 12 petal lotus
- Color: Bright Emerald Green
- Sanskrit Mantra – Sound: YAM (Yummmmmm)

The Heart Chakra is the wellspring of love in all forms, and the powerhouse of forgiveness, open-heartedness, compassion and empathy. It is the home to 'openness' and governs the ability to give and receive unconditional love, and in turn is the open door to unbounded, joyful connection to God, the universe, the Source of All.

His Holiness the Dali Lama said:

"Love and Compassion are necessities, not Luxuries. Without them, humanity cannot survive."

That being true, how much more important is it for you to learn the art of allowing love and compassion for yourself? To heal the Heart Chakra is a sacred step to healing the world. By healing and then releasing a lifetimes worth of constricted energy and stepping into unbounded joy is not only serving your Higher Self but serving the global interwoven web of humanity. As the great Sufi poet, Rumi wrote: "Your Heart knows the way. Run in that direction." After learning to clear and release negative energy contained in your Heart Chakra, return to it routinely.

Dysfunctional thought patterns involving Heart Chakra: Lack of self-love and self-fulfillment, depression, anxiety, grief, feelings of betrayal, self-abandonment. Broken-heartedness, isolation, and unworthiness manifest through energy blocks in this pivotal energy center.

Truth Hint: *Isolation is common when the Heart Chakra is severely blocked. Do you find when you are lacking confidence or feeling unsure and without momentum you choose to isolate yourself? Do you feel more comfortable being alone and finding excuses to hide or withdraw when you have low energy? I fell victim to this behavior during my first cat life. If I didn't feel 'perfect' and 'on top of things,' I hid myself away. I only engaged with others when I felt good. I became a master at presenting only my very best self. I did not live authentically. I did not understand that we are all imperfect and that by being authentic and 'showing up' even in a state of imperfection was not only healthier but more appealing to others. I was obvious that my 'perfection' routine was grating on others nerves. I had the insane notion that being less than 'perfect' was letting others down.*

If you find yourself becoming isolated or in a state of perpetual perfection-seeking, please place special attention on healing your Heart Chakra.

The 5th Energy Center: <u>The Throat Chakra is the Vishuddha</u>, which in Sanskrit means 'Purification' and is the first of the three spiritual chakras. This is the 5th Chakra and Powerhouse of your Personal Truth.

- Location: Sits directly in the middle of your throat.
- Symbol: 16 petal lotus
- Color: Bright Cerulean or Sky Blue
- Sanskrit Mantra – Sound: HAM (Hummmmmmm)

This Chakra is the home of your personal truth, your own unique voice, and your personal integrity. This energy center is the wellspring of personal expression, openness, communication and personal conviction. From the place of

Vishuddha, you communicate your deep and unique wisdom.

Dysfunctional thought patterns involving Throat Chakra: Lack of direction, uncertainty in thoughts and speech, inability to set boundaries, inability to stand up for convictions. When throat chakra is blocked or out of balance it creates a barrier in pursuing your destiny. It may create a tendency to be less than authentic and truthful. You may feel unable to grow and live to your potential because you will choose to play small and not let your inner voice and wisdom ring through.

Truth Hint: *Do you find you are constantly clearing your throat when you are speaking to others? In my first cat life I had a chronic hair ball condition. I didn't think much of it at the time. It seemed normal for cats to have hair balls perpetually stuck in their throat. But that isn't true, we don't need to create annoying hairballs any more than you do. I was unconsciously creating a physical condition in which my Inner Being was attempting to bring me clarity. What I was experiencing was a blocked 5th Chakra. My body created the hairball as a red flag so that I would clue in that something was very wrong. The problem was I didn't clue in at the time so I suffered mightily. If you are experiencing awkward habits when speaking, you too may have a blocked Vishuddha.*

Do you suffer from neck and shoulder pain or carry tension at the base of your scalp? You may not be standing in your personal truth. As mentioned before, our body is masterful at calling out in the area needing attention.

When I cleared my 5th Chakra I realized I can call on clarity and invincibility at any moment and when speaking my personal truth I have no fear. It takes conviction and confidence. But you gain this conviction and confidence naturally when you clear and open the Vishuddha. It also helps to give up caring about what anyone thinks of you too! Stop. Caring. Today.

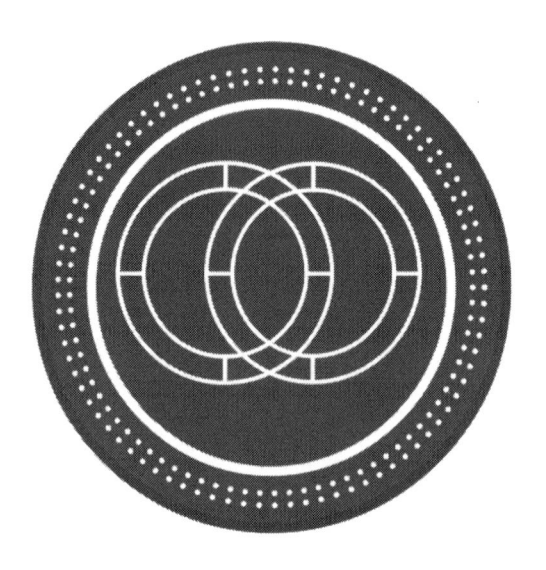

The 6th Energy Center: The 3rd Eye Chakra is the Anja, which in Sanskrit means 'to perceive' or 'to know.' This is the 6th Chakra and is home to your intuition, and "seat of oneness."

- Location: Sits directly in the space between your eyebrows.

- Symbol: a lotus with 2 large petals. This Chakra has two petals because it is linked to the pituitary gland which consists of two parts, the anterior and the posterior lobes as well as the two hemispheres of the brain. It is also associated with the endocrine and lymphatic system.

- Color: Bright Indigo (Dark) Blue

- Sanskrit Mantra – Sound: SHAM (Shummmmmmm)

This Chakra is the home of your personal life experience culminating in your personal intelligence and experienced through insight and instinct. Anja is your inner voice which guides your choices. It is home to your deeper understanding and most ancient awareness. It is your seat of intuition, clairvoyance, guidance and inner wisdom. This Chakra governs your relationship with the spiritual world and is your powerhouse of divine benevolence. A clear Anja provides for messenger dreams, where your inner wisdom, the voice of your soul, may instruct you on your path.

Dysfunctional thought patterns involving the 3rd Eye Chakra: Lack of hope, restlessness, inability to believe in optimistic outcomes. A blocked 6th Chakra will cause an inability to seek higher truths and deeper understandings of spiritual connectedness. This may lead to depression or general feelings of being morose and unfulfilled.

Truth Hint: Dreams are an amazing tool to assist in gaining deep clarity. When sleeping, you are absent of resistance and your mind untethers from the conscious realm and is open to the insight manifested when speaking to your Higher Self. You don't have to wait for a full night's sleep to access inner wisdom. If I need to have an answer fast I take a nap. I give myself permission to cut loose from whatever I perceive my 'doing' must be at this moment and I go find a nice place to drift off and reconnect with my soul.

When I find that I am 'stuck' and without momentum or if I find I am attached to pervasive upstream thoughts and creating more resistance by cycling a certain thought pattern within my mind, I know it's time for a nap. I make sure to allow my mind to clear to the best of my ability. I focus on bringing my mind to a very general place and I ask for assistance from my guides or angels. I ask that the perceiver aspect of my Anja receive all that the universe and my higher self-wishes to bestow. When I awaken I feel not only rested but on target. It's as if I were given a divine download for any resolution I may have been seeking. The beauty of this tool is that it brings clarity and focus through effortlessness and divine rest.

The 7th Energy Center: <u>The Crown Chakra is the Sahasrara</u> (or Sahaswara,) and in Sanskrit translates to thousand fold (and often referred to as the thousand petal lotus) and is the purest representation of connectedness with the spiritual domain, Source or God. It is the essence of total enlightenment.

- Location: Sits above the top of your skull approximately 3 inches directly in the center.
- Symbol: a thousand petal Lotus.
- Color: Bright Ultra Violet
- Sanskrit Mantra – Sound: OM (Ommmmmmm)

This Chakra is the seat of Divine Consciousness. It is a portal to the universe of transcendent thought and peace. This

Energy Center personifies the attributes of bliss, grace, beauty, serenity, and oneness with all that is and ever will be. When opened and restored your memory of who you really are, the breath of Spirit in a human disguise will engulf you with centeredness, feeling of wholeness and connected to eternity.

Sahasrara is the reaching of a point of consciousness wherein, you realize as the poet Rumi states "you are not just a drop of water in the ocean you are the mighty ocean in the drop." This 7th Chakra represents the realm of unbounded awareness, the resting place of tranquility that in turn is the intricately interwoven web of the divine.

Here you will experience an inextricable connection to the Creator of the universe and the wisdom of the ages. Unattainable? Perhaps it is for most of us as a permanent construct. But it *is* possible to have moments, seconds, even nano-seconds where you cross a veil of perception and align with eternal knowing through the Sahasrara. And it's worth it!

Dysfunctional thought patterns involving Crown Chakra would include megalomania, exceedingly superficial mindset, or even a Messiah complex. You are likely to find people with blocked Crown Chakras will have severely closed minds, unable to comprehend the thought of listening to another's opinion, preferring to be right rather than know the truth.

The Crown Chakra is elusive. It is usually closed to at least some degree, otherwise, we would be communing with our soul and divinity all the time, unable to live fruitfully in this temporal world. But when this level of 'oneness' is even glimpsed, it is a manifestation of grace always to be pursued by those on the path to deeper understanding.

Truth Hint*: The opening and clearing of the Sahasrara may result in the feeling of a rushing breeze extending from the top of your head. If you experience this, you are being gifted beyond measure. Many practitioners of energy healing liken this sensation to the realization of the Holy Spirt or Breath of Life. It is called prana in Sanskrit and ki in Japanese meaning the breath of the universe, a cosmic force which penetrates all things. For Christians this rush of wind will symbolize the Holy Spirit who fills all things with this breath of life bestowing love, giving wisdom and bringing joy and peace.*

Part Three

Healing and Clearing Your Energy Centers

The 8 Day Journey

Day 1
Bringing in the Light

The first day of your simple 8 Day Journey is all about preparation. But it is easy preparation. You have already prepared your Divine Space. Today is meant to prepare your body, mind and heart to open, focus, heal and release during the next seven days.

You begin by getting acquainted with your body intimately and this means learning to feel and perceive the feeling sensations your body presents in any given situation. We all have good feeling sensations and not so good feeling sensations. Learning to recognize what specific feeling sensation your physical body is presenting is a powerful tool that can provide you with a deeper energy healing experience. Discovering how to feel into your body deeply can be accomplished through the simple grounding exercise below. For some of you, this may be the first time you have ever traversed so deeply into your physical body. However, I guarantee that learning to feel your own physical body intimately will help you to reach deeper into your energetic system to allow for easier clearing and healing.

Your Body does not lie...

In fact, your body is a truth detector, sort of like a built-in GPS system. Learning to feel your body sensation in any situation provides a springboard to successful energy healing. If more people were mindful of their bodies throughout their day to day life, and recognized the feeling sensations being conjured by the body to get their attention, most would 'magically' avoid life's tricky potholes. You can use this tool day in and day out, during all waking hours and in every situation. When you are aware of a message your body is sharing, such as a fluttering in the middle of your chest or ringing ears or a nagging scratchy throat you can bring this awareness into your energy healing for clearing. The following Grounding Exercise will help you learn how to become aware of your body so you can start to pick up any messages it is sending you.

Grounding Exercise

After you have made yourself comfortable, either lying down or sitting up straight but relaxed (I like lying down best), gently close your eyes. Make an intention to be right here, right now. Simply listen to the silence for a few seconds. You may even hear your heartbeat – which is something many of us never take the time to do.

Now, intentionally and slowly inhale a full breath through your nose expanding your rib cage and hold it for 4 seconds. Slowly exhale this breath through the mouth for 6 seconds. Repeat this sequence 4 times to oxygenate your entire body with universal breath. Why do I call it universal breath? Because every living thing takes in the same oxygen. Every one of us, including all animals, plants and trees have this in common.

With your eyes closed, begin to breathe normally and gently press your feet into the floor and feel your feet. Feel your toes (or if you're a cat feel you paw pads and gently click your claws into the floor.) Differentiate your toes mentally. Take a few seconds to note 'Oh yes, I have 5 toes on the right and 5 toes on the left foot' by wiggling them and bringing them into your awareness.

Beginning with the big toe on your right foot, visualize your circulatory system. Visualize the blood, which courses through your body 24/7, and trace it from your Big toe, through your foot, up your shin, and into your thigh. Don't rush when doing this. Go slowly and visualize your blood actually moving up your limb. Now take it up further, into your pelvis moving up your spine, through your heart and into your chest. Continue to breathe in a regular manner. Make sure you do not hold your breath.

Continue to follow the flow of blood over your right shoulder and down the front side of your right arm, past the bicep, to the forearm and down to your fingers. Keep breathing. Now follow it up the backside of your hand down your wrist and up the underside of your arm. Keep breathing.

The blood should now be flowing into your armpit. Continue to follow it up the right side of your neck over your face to the top of your head. As it climbs the right side of your scalp let it run over to the left side, bring it down your face visualizing the internal structure of your face, your eyes, and nose, and bring it down to the left side of your neck. Follow the traveling blood circulating through your shoulder and down the front of your left arm, past your bicep and down the forearm to the tips of your fingers. Keep breathing.

Follow the blood up the back of your hand, over your wrist and up your arm depositing into the armpit. Keep breathing. The blood is now circulating back to your spine. Follow it travel down the spine and to your pelvis. Visualize the circulating blood coursing through your left thigh, down your shin to your left foot and ending at your left big toe.

You have now completed a full body activation. You are mentally and physically aware of your entire body. Congratulations.

It is time to Bring in the Light

This first day of healing is all about bringing in the light through your cranium and flushing your body with brilliant healing white light. Before we do this, I want you to feel into your body. Are there any emotions coming up with this new adventure, either positive or negative?

If there are, what are they? This is a good time to jot this information into your journal. But sometimes it is very difficult to put into words what you may be experiencing. You don't need to be able to verbalize with clarity and precision what you are feeling; especially when this is new and you have no clue on what you're feeling or how to describe it. That is normal.

In your journal, note the emotions you are feeling. Just write down words that express the emotion you are feeling at the moment. Such as: 'giddy, excited, fearless' Or, 'frightened, anxious, nauseous.' Whatever you are feeling it is important to note it so you can work with your specific energy centers as you become more comfortable with energy healing.

The emotion you are feeling at any given time is an indication of your current energy frequency. If you are having positive emotions, your energy is clear and vibrant. If you are having emotions related to feeling anxiety, tension, sadness or frustration, it is critical to be able to identify this too as you are not aligned energetically with your Higher Self. There is nothing to be ashamed of when negative emotions arise. Having negative emotions is natural. We all have the same feelings from time to time. The part you want to understand is that you do not have to fall victim to the emotions. You can pinpoint the emotion and take it into energy healing for release. Use your body's GPS to feel the sensation and find its location. Spend time with the sensation and tie it to your emotion. What does it feel like? Try to describe it using short adjectives. Some examples might be hot, sharp, heavy, excited, joyful, anxious, and icy.

Feeling the Body Sensation

Here is a quick personal example of becoming attuned to your body sensations. In my first cat life, I had generalized bouts of anxiety hit me unexpectedly. I could have been humming away in my bedroom to my favorite song, bright eyed and bushy tailed, happy as a lark and then leave the room and as I leaped my way toward the door on my way to the kitchen, without having a different conscious thought, a sense of impending doom would wash over me as if a black cape weighing forty pounds had been draped over my little kitty shoulders. It felt heavy, dark, and icky.

What were my emotions and how did they manifest in my body?

My heart would begin to beat rapidly, I would break out in a cold sweat and my lovely fur coat would be soaked, then my gut would hit the floor. So what happened? I was not aligned with my Higher Self. In that moment, I subconsciously had a lot of negative thoughts and limiting beliefs– but they were hidden from my awareness.

But my body was speaking truth. My body was screaming out to get my attention. My body wanted me to start paying attention. My body was sending up a red flag alert that I was not following my bliss, I was off track and I was dissolving on the inside. The problem was back then I didn't know listening to my body for clues was important and I didn't have a clue about energy healing. It wasn't until I was reborn that I learned this ancient modality for healing.

Today, if I were experiencing those body sensations I would immediately drop in and listen intently. I would use the adjectives 'impending doom, heavy, black, and icky' to develop a name for my emotions and the story my thoughts were conspiring to conjure. I would probably call it my 'Big Black Shroud' story and realize it is a series of uninvited, unconscious thoughts. I would immediately bring it to energy healing for clearing paying special attention to the first three Chakras and the Heart Chakra.

You have the opportunity to learn, here and now, what slipped my notice in my first life. Learn to listen to your body. It is speaking to you all the time. Take the emotions and the feeling sensation into your energy clearing for deep healing.

Exercise: White Light Visualization

I offer this additional exercise to help you feel into your body and generate stronger focus is the White Light Visualization exercise. This exercise helps to stimulate a sense of calm focus by incorporating a thorough body scan.

Energy Healing Made Simple – Om Kitty

In your divine space, put on your favorite meditation music and light either incense or an aromatherapy candle. Either lying on the floor or sitting comfortable, yet straight, in a chair, close your eyes. Begin to breathe in a universal breath as you did at the beginning of the grounding exercise, in for four counts and out for six counts.

Visualize a glass cylindrical container running through your body from the top of your head to the base of your spine. Gently place your hand's palm up on the top of your legs.

Now visualize a brilliant white light from the heavens entering the top of your head piercing an Ultra-violet cloud contained within the glass cylinder. Stay with this visualization, concentrating on the light penetrating the Ultra-violet cloud. Hold this visualization for the count of ten.

Move the white beam of light downward by mentally pushing the light to the area of your eyebrows. Let the white light pierce an Indigo colored cloud contained within the glass cylinder. Maintain the visualization, concentrating on the light penetrating the Indigo cloud. Hold this visualization for the count of ten.

Move the white beam of light downward, this is achieved by mentally pushing the light to the area of your throat. Let the white light pierce a Sky Blue colored cloud contained within the glass cylinder. Maintain the visualization, concentrating on the light penetrating the Sky Blue cloud. Hold this visualization for the count of ten.

Move the white beam of light downward by mentally pushing the light to the area of your heart. Let the white light pierce an emerald colored cloud contained within the glass cylinder. Maintain the visualization, concentrating on the light penetrating the emerald cloud. Hold this visualization for the count of ten.

Move the white beam of light downward by mentally pushing the light to the area of your solar plexus region. Let the while light pierce a canary yellow colored cloud contained within the glass cylinder. Maintain the visualization, concentrating on the light penetrating the yellow cloud. Hold this visualization for the count of ten.

Move the white beam of light downward by mentally pushing the light to the area of your sacral region. Let the while light pierce a bright orange colored cloud contained within the glass cylinder. Maintain the visualization, concentrating on the light penetrating the orange cloud. Hold this visualization for the count of ten.

Finally, move the white beam of light downward by mentally pushing the light to the area of your coccyx region. Let the while light pierce a bright ruby red colored cloud contained within the glass cylinder. Maintain the visualization, concentrating on the light penetrating the red cloud. Hold this visualization for the count of ten.

Now, after holding the white light at the Root Chakra for ten seconds mentally push the white light out through your toes.

As the white light leaves your toes, visualize white feathers rising up into the air and disappearing. The white feathers represent energy that no longer serves you.

Now, it is time to close your Energy Centers since they have been purified. This will enable you to move throughout your day without allowing unnecessary negative energy to penetrate through to your bright and shiny chakras. Go to the top of your head and visualize a lit Ultra-violet candle and blow it out. Do the same with each chakra, visualizing a lit candle in the corresponding color, indigo, sky blue and so on, and blow it out. You are ready to take on the day feeling invincible and clear.

You are now ready to move forward to the next 7 Days of your healing journey.

Day 2
The Root Chakra

The Muladhara

The Root Chakra is also known as the Base Chakra as it is located at the base of the spine. This base energy center is the seat of your most elementary and primal needs including survival, safety, family, and belief systems. It is the system which grounds you in the physical dimension. Anatomically, it governs the lower extremities including feet and knees as well as bones, blood.

A healthy unblocked Root Chakra will allow for centeredness. You innately know the universe has your back. You will feel safe, secure and included. You will trust the world to be your ally. You will trust others and know with certainty all is perfectly working out for you as always.

A blocked Root Chakra will leave you feeling ungrounded, lost, and insecure, estranged from others, clingy, afraid, and suspicious, with possibly fear of abandonment. You may feel no one understands you or you are not loved or supported. You may feel alone. You will generally mistrust others and the world in general.

To Clear, Heal, and Activate
Your Root Chakra

In your divine space, after conducting your daily ritual settle in and state this intention:

"I intend to engage in the healing of my Root Chakra. I call on all benevolent Love to come to my aid. I acknowledge my deep desire to heal. I release all negative energy that bars me from living in complete serenity, assured in the knowledge I am safe, I am secure, I am loved."

Now, close your eyes and put your hands on the region of your Root Chakra. Begin to breathe in the universal breathe as instructed in the grounding exercise, in for four counts and out for six counts.

Returning to your normal breathing rhythm, visualize a brilliant white light from the heavens entering your feet and stopping at the Root Chakra creating a warm tingly sensation in your lower extremities. Visualize a bright ruby red 4 petal lotus appearing. See the lotus spinning clockwise as it prepares to heal. Hold this visualization for the count of ten. You are activating your root chakra. Continue to breathe normally.

Escalate your healing now by silently repeating this Mantra: "*I am safe, I am whole, I am healed.*" Continue to repeat the mantra for three minutes. Repeat the mantra silently over and over as you visualize the red lotus spinning clockwise faster and faster.

Bringing in the white light, mentally move the light down pushing the red lotus down from your coccyx region and out through your feet. Now visualize the red lotus opening up releasing a stream of white feathers. Mentally follow these white feathers upward towards heaven. The feathers represent the expelled negative energy that no longer serves you.

Now it is time to close your root chakra as it is now purified and activated. Gently visualize a bright red lit candle and mindfully state: "*I am safe, I am whole, I am healed.*" Blow the candle out.

Go out and conqueror you day knowing you are taking care of yourself. All really is well.

Day 3
The Sacral Chakra

Svadhisthana

The Sacral Chakra is located at the region of your hip bones and is associated with our sexuality, sensuality, and creativity. Anatomically, it is related to the reproductive system, ovaries and testes as well as bladder, kidneys, and intestines.

Our interpersonal relationships are governed by the Sacral chakra.

A healthy, unblocked Sacral Chakra will allow for passionate friendships and romantic relationships, strong interpersonal skills, ability to pursue desires, enhanced creativity, and overall general happiness.

An unhealthy or blocked Sacral Chakra will cause an imbalance in relationships. You may feel disempowered, weak, or overly shy. Fear of interpersonal interaction may occur or, you may focus on what others perception of you might be. You may experience unnecessary guilt or shame. You may have a hard time believing you are loveable.

To Clear, Heal and Activate Your Sacral Chakra

In your divine space, after conducting your daily ritual, settle in and state this intention:

"I intend to engage in the healing of my Sacral Chakra. I call on all benevolent love to come to my aid. I acknowledge my deep desire to heal. I release all negative energy that bars me from living in complete serenity, assured in the knowledge I am desirable, I am creative, I am engaging, I am loved."

Now close your eyes and put your hands on the region of your Sacral Chakra. Begin to breathe in universal breathe as instructed in the grounding exercise, in for four counts and out for six counts.

Returning to your normal breathing rhythm, visualize a brilliant white light from the heavens entering your feet and stopping at the Sacral Chakra, creating a warm tingly sensation from your hips downwards. Visualize a bright orange 6 petal lotus appearing. See the lotus spinning clockwise as it prepares to heal. Hold this visualization for the count of ten. You are activating your sacral chakra. Continue to breathe normally.

Escalate your healing now by silently repeating this Mantra: "I am creative, I am worthy, I am whole, I am healed." Continue to repeat the mantra for three minutes. Repeat the mantra silently over and over as you visualize the orange lotus spinning clockwise faster and faster.

Bringing in the white light mentally move the light down pushing the orange lotus down from your hip region and out through your feet. Now visualize the orange lotus opening up releasing a stream of white feathers. Mentally follow these white feathers upward towards heaven. The feathers represent the expelled negative energy that no longer serves you.

Now it is time to close your Sacral Chakra as it is now purified and activated. Gently visualize a bright orange lit candle and mindfully state: "I am creative, I am worthy, I am whole, I am healed." Blow the candle out.

Go out and be creative and engage in today knowing bliss and happiness is yours to have. All really is well.

Day 4
The Solar Plexus Chakra

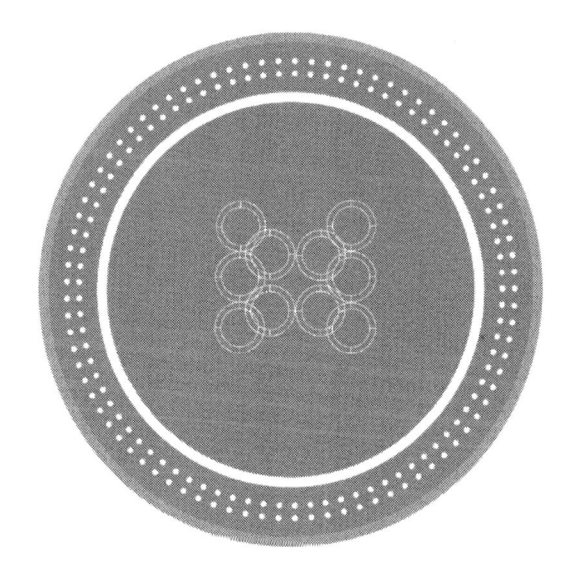

Manipura

The Solar Plexus Chakra is our emotional powerhouse. We react, positively or negatively, according to the health of this energy base. Anatomically, this chakra relates to our adrenal system, our digestive system and the upper lumbar region of our spine. This is where we receive our gut instincts.

A healthy and balanced 3rd Chakra will allow for self-confidence, exuberance, self-assuredness, calm resolution of problems and overall respect for others.

An unhealthy and blocked Sacral Chakra will manifest in low self-esteem, general lack of energy, victimization mindset, a general 'lack' mentality manifesting as poor finances and unhealthy relationships.

To Clear, Heal and Activate
Your Solar Plexus Chakra

In your divine space, after conducting your daily ritual settle in and state this intention:

> *"I intend to engage in the healing of my Solar Plexus Chakra. I call on all benevolent love to come to my aid. I acknowledge my deep desire to heal. I release all negative energy that bars me from living in complete serenity, assured in the knowledge I am powerful, I am assured, I am loved."*

Now close your eyes and put your hands on the region of your Solar Plexus Chakra. Begin to breathe in universal breathe as instructed in the grounding exercise, in for four counts and out for six counts.

Returning to your normal breathing rhythm, visualize a brilliant white light from the heavens entering your feet and stopping at the Solar Plexus Chakra creating a warm tingly sensation from your rib cage down. Visualize a bright yellow 8 petal lotus appearing. See the lotus spinning clockwise as it prepares to heal. Hold this visualization for the count of ten. You are activating your Solar Plexus Chakra. Continue to breathe normally.

Escalate your healing now by silently repeating this Mantra: "I am powerful, I am vibrant, I am healed." Continue to repeat the mantra for three minutes. Repeat the mantra silently over and over as you visualize the yellow lotus spinning clockwise faster and faster.

Bringing in the white light mentally move the light down pushing the yellow lotus down from your rib cage and out through your feet. Now visualize the yellow lotus opening up releasing a stream of white feathers. Mentally follow these white feathers upward towards heaven. The feathers represent the expelled negative energy that no longer serves you.

Now it is time to close your Solar Plexus Chakra as it is now purified and activated. Gently visualize a bright yellow lit candle and mindfully state: "I am invincible, I am self-assured, I am healed." Blow the candle out.

Go out and be in your personal power, confident and exuberant knowing anything you desire can be yours. Trust in your personal power and meet your intentions through effortless connection to the universal life force. All really is well.

Day 5
Heart Chakra

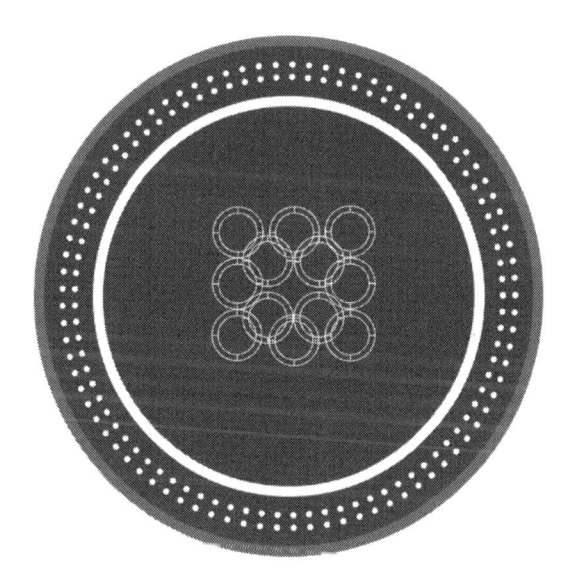

Anahatta

The Heart Chakra is the mid-point energy center, the portal to the spiritual realms and the gateway to the earth linked realms. This fourth Chakra is the seat of love, human and divine. This Energy Center governs the higher attributes of kindness, generosity, empathy, sincerity, compassion. Anatomically this Chakra represents the heart, circulatory system, the immune system, the shoulders, and arms as well as the thymus glands.

The Heart Chakra is a special place of healing. It is the dwelling place of purification and the well-spring of flowing love. This is the abode of soul-centeredness.

A healthy and balanced Heart Chakra will allow for increased capacity to love and be loved. It will result in optimally knowing you are benevolently loved by the Source of all love. You will have natural empathy and compassion and a greater sense of wellbeing. You rest assured in the knowledge that all in the universe is well and the 'manager of the cosmos' is at the wheel of the ship.

An unhealthy or blocked Heart Chakra will result in fears of rejection, feeling unloved or uncared for, increased insecurity. You may feel you must perform to be loved. You may fall into the trap of doing everything for everyone else while receiving very little in return. You may give of yourself to the point of destruction. You may feel a grieving sensation or a loss of bonding. You may be depleted in the area of self-love and self-care.

To Clear, Heal and Activate Your Heart Chakra

In your divine space, after conducting your daily ritual settle in and state this intention:

"I intend to engage in the healing of my Heart Chakra. I call on all benevolent love to come to my aid. I acknowledge my deep desire to heal. I release all negative energy that bars me from living in complete serenity, assured in the knowledge I am love, I know love, I am loved."

Now close your eyes and put your hands on the region of your Heart Chakra. Begin to breathe in universal breathe as instructed in the grounding exercise, in for four counts and out for six counts.

Returning to your normal breathing rhythm, visualize a brilliant white light from the heavens entering your feet and stopping at the Heart Chakra creating a warm tingly sensation from the middle of your chest down. Visualize a bright green 12 petal lotus appearing. See the lotus spinning clockwise as it prepares to heal. Hold this visualization for the count of ten. You are activating your heart chakra. Continue to breathe normally.

Escalate your healing now by silently repeating this Mantra: "I know love, I have love, I am love, I am healed." Continue to repeat the mantra for three minutes. Repeat the mantra silently over and over as you visualize the green lotus spinning clockwise faster and faster.

Bringing in the white light mentally move the light down pushing the green lotus down from the middle of your chest and slowly all the way down and out through your feet. Now visualize the green lotus opening up releasing a stream of white feathers. Mentally follow these white feathers upward towards heaven. The feathers represent the expelled negative energy that no longer serves you.

Now, it is time to close your Heart Chakra as it is now purified and activated. Gently visualize a bright green lit candle and mindfully state: "I am love, All is well, I am healed." Blow the candle out.

Go out and be in love with yourself, with others, with your job, with your living environment. Know today that all really is well.

Day 6
Throat Chakra

Vishudda

The Throat Chakra is the seat of personal integrity and truth. This fifth energy center is the resting place of self-expression and expression to others. It is home to our truth, our personal convictions and governs our internal guidance system. Anatomically, the Throat Chakra represents the upper chest, neck, nasal cavity and passages, throat, mouth, ears, and two glands: the thyroid and parathyroid.

A healthy, balanced Throat Chakra allows for easy, strong and effective communication. When the Throat Chakra is balanced, you will feel strong and assured knowing you speak your personal truth. You conduct yourself with confidence knowing you are heard and understood, thereby your needs are being met.

An unhealthy or blocked Throat Chakra results in ineffective speech. You may perceive no one is listening or taking you seriously. You may be over critical of others and yourself. You may be unable to freely express yourself because your personal truth is being energetically blocked. You may seem either timid or you may seem to not make sense. Others will have a hard time believing you. You may even resort to lying. You may notice that you have a constant 'catch' or 'tickle' in your throat. Your speech may not be clear and you might mumble. You may be prone to raise your voice or yell a lot. You might have fits of loud anger.

To Clear, Heal and Activate
Your Throat Chakra

In your divine space, after conducting your daily ritual settle in and state this intention:

"I intend to engage in the healing of my Throat Chakra. I call on all benevolent love to come to my aid. I acknowledge my deep desire to heal. I release all negative energy that bars me from living in complete serenity, assured in the knowledge I speak truth, I know my convictions, I am heard, I am loved."

Now close your eyes and put your hands on the region of your Throat Chakra. Begin to breathe in universal breathe as instructed in the grounding exercise, in for four counts and out for six counts.

Returning to your normal breathing rhythm, visualize a brilliant white light from the heavens entering your feet and stopping at the Throat Chakra creating a warm tingly sensation from the middle of your neck down. Visualize a bright Sky Blue 16 petal lotus appearing. See the lotus spinning clockwise as it prepares to heal. Hold this visualization for the count of ten. You are activating your Throat Chakra. Continue to breathe normally.

Escalate your healing now by silently repeating this Mantra: "I speak truth, I know truth, I am truth, I am healed." Continue to repeat the mantra for three minutes. Repeat the mantra silently over and over as you visualize the Sky Blue lotus spinning clockwise faster and faster.

Bringing in the white light mentally move the light down pushing the Sky Blue lotus down from the middle of your throat and slowly down and out through your feet. Now visualize the Sky Blue lotus opening up releasing a stream of white feathers. Mentally follow these white feathers upward towards heaven. The feathers represent the expelled negative energy that no longer serves you.

Now it is time to close your Throat Chakra as it is now purified and activated. Gently visualize a bright Sky Blue lit candle and mindfully state: "I speak truth, I know truth, all is well, I am healed." Blow the candle out.

Go out and walk in your own personal truth. Be free to be your authentic self and let people meet the real you. All really is well.

Day 7
3rd Eye Chakra

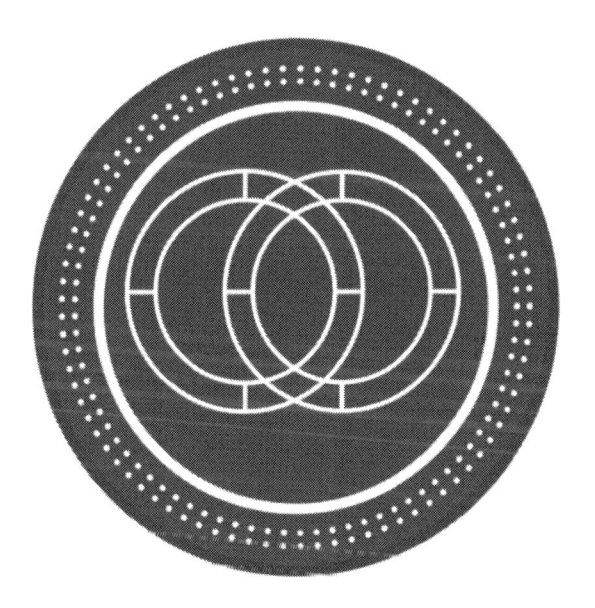

Anja

The Anja or 3rd Eye Chakra is the 'Perceiver'. Here you connect with your inner knowing, your highest level of personal wisdom. This Chakra governs the dual hemispheres of our brain, our left and our right, our logical and creative capacities as well as the lymphatic and endocrine systems. This is the home to our intuitive sense, our sixth sense, our psychic abilities and our ability to grasp eternity.

A balanced Anja allows for the super-power of intuition and greater sense of clarity and focus. Your sixth sense will perk up and you will feel an energetic alignment with animals, nature and humans as well. You feel connected to your Higher Self. You choose to align with health, happiness, and joy.

An unbalanced or blocked Anja will result in a feeling of disconnect and being ungrounded. You may unwittingly perceive things not as they truly are and therefore create unnecessary suffering for yourself. You may feel you are flitting through the world with no direction, unguided and disposable. You may seem lost and unfocused. You may not be able to resist the lure of fast talkers and sly perpetrators. You may distrust your intuitive voice.

To Clear, Heal and Activate Your 3rd Eye Chakra

In your divine space, after conducting your daily ritual settle in and state this intention:

"I intend to engage in the healing of my 3rd Eye Chakra. I call on all benevolent love to come to my aid. I acknowledge my deep desire to heal. I release all negative energy that bars me from living in complete serenity, assured in the knowledge I perceive, I discern, I know at a deeper level, I am loved."

Now close your eyes and put your hands on the region of your 3rd Eye Chakra. Begin to breathe in universal breath as instructed in the grounding exercise, in for four counts and out for six counts.

Returning to your normal breathing rhythm, visualize a brilliant white light from the heavens entering your feet and stopping at the 3rd Eye Chakra creating a warm tingly sensation from the eyebrow down. Visualize a bright Indigo-blue 2 petal lotus appearing. See the lotus spinning clockwise as it prepares to heal. Hold this visualization for the count of ten. You are activating your 3rd Eye chakra. Continue to breathe normally.

Escalate your healing now by silently repeating this Mantra: "I perceive, I sense, I intuit, I am healed." Continue to repeat the mantra for three minutes. Repeat the mantra silently over and over as you visualize the indigo-blue lotus spinning clockwise faster and faster.

Bringing in the white light mentally move the light down pushing the Indigo-blue lotus down from your eyebrow and slowly all the way down and out through your feet. Now visualize the Indigo-blue lotus opening up releasing a stream of white feathers. Mentally follow these white feathers upward towards heaven. The feathers represent the expelled negative energy that no longer serves you.

Now it is time to close your 3rd Eye Chakra as it is now purified and activated. Gently visualize a dark Indigo-blue lit candle and mindfully state: "I am connected, I know, I am certain, All is well, I am healed." Blow the candle out.

Walk into the world today feeling the eternal connection of benevolent love, knowing that all really is well.

Day 8
Crown Chakra

Sahasrara

The Sahasrara or Crown Chakra allows for serenity, ease, a greater inherent understanding, calm reflection and the ability to walk at ease with oneself and with others. A healthy Crown Chakra provides clarity, certainty, ability to allow abundance and a natural flow to the order of things. You know with certainty that you are being supported and you are connected to benevolent love. The Crown Chakra is the seat of universal energy and connectivity with the Source of All ushering in heightened wisdom and bliss. Inherently, this energy center supports the strong, intuitive understanding that you are part of an incomparable unity, a connection to a divine wholeness.

An unhealthy or blocked Crown Chakra would manifest feelings of being lost, without connection and a general inability to relax or have enjoyment in the living of life. You may even grieve for connection.

To Clear, Heal and Activate Your Crown Chakra

In your divine space, after conducting your daily ritual settle in and state this intention:

"I intend to engage in the healing of my Crown Chakra. I call on all benevolent love to come to my aid. I acknowledge my deep desire to heal. I release all negative energy that bars me from living in complete serenity, assured in the knowledge I am connected, I am certain, I am relaxed, I am loved."

Now close your eyes and put your hands on the region of your Crown Chakra, at the top of your head. Begin to breathe in universal breathe as instructed in the grounding exercise, in for four counts and out for six counts.

Returning to your normal breathing rhythm, visualize a brilliant white light from the heavens entering your feet, moving up your body and stopping at the Crown Chakra creating a warm tingly sensation from the top of your skull and down through your entire body. Visualize an Ultraviolet thousand petal lotus appearing. See the lotus spinning clockwise as it prepares to heal. Hold this visualization for the count of ten. You are activating your Crown chakra. Continue to breathe normally.

Escalate your healing now by silently repeating this Mantra: "I am connected, I am certain, I am complete, I am healed." Continue to repeat the mantra for three minutes. Repeat the mantra silently over and over as you visualize the Ultra-violet lotus spinning clockwise faster and faster.

Bringing in the white light mentally move the light down pushing the Ultra-violet lotus down from just above your head and slowly all the way down and out through your feet. Now visualize the ultra-violet lotus opening up releasing a stream of white feathers. Mentally follow these white feathers upward towards heaven. The feathers represent the expelled negative energy that no longer serves you.

Now it is time to close your Crown Chakra as it is now purified and activated. Gently visualize a Ultra-violet lit candle and mindfully state: "I am one with Source, the eternal flame of love, creator of all that is, all is well, I am healed." Blow the candle out.

Walk into the world today feeling the eternal connection of benevolent love, knowing that all really is well.

The Next Step ...

The value experienced in Energy Healing comes from commitment and practice.

After you have completed this simple 8 Day Journey consider making this healing a permanent part of your life. You can choose to focus on one specific energy center at a time or perform a full sweep of the entire energetic system.

Additionally, keep your eye's peeled for the entire OM Kitty Book Series, coming soon, where I'll be taking you further on your own personal **Spiritual Awakening With a Twist** adventure. You can also find my daily missives, musings and more Truth Hints here. Just copy this link into your browser.

http://wp.me/P5D95B-jQ

A Note of Gratitude

I sincerely thank you for reading my fist book in this series and for allowing me this space in your life. It is my deepest hope that you have enjoyed my writing and hopefully gained some information that resonates with you at your highest level. We can be as healed, as grateful, as abundant and as blessed as we choose to be if we choose to deliberately align with our soul's gentle whisper. Remember to breathe, feel in to your body for signals, line up energetically and be brave knowing that the universe really is conspiring to usher you into your best life.

Hey by the way! Did you remember to download your beautiful **Bonus Gifts** found at the top of this book? I've put together this little bonus package of other fun things you can consider implementing once you have followed through with this Energy Healing and Chakra Activation. These bonus gifts will aid in helping you feel comfortable, confident and clear.

If you didn't download your FREE - OM Kitty's Awesome Kit-and-Caboodles Bonus Gift Package at the top of the book you may do so now. Just copy this link into your browser.

http://wp.me/P5D95B-lA!

The following quote, although not specifically about energy healing, is a lovely explanation why incorporating beneficial healing modalities of any kind into your lifestyle is a good thing. Dr. Martha Beck is an important mentor to my own personal development and she shares that any form of goodness, in other words, any modality to strengthen your clarity, wellbeing, and alignment with a benevolent creator, should be a welcome addition to your personal tool kit.

"For now, it's enough for me to think that angels, or for that matter any forms of goodness, function like water; they run into any opening they are given. There may be some people who are born open, who soak up goodness like sponges and leave traces of it on everything they touch. But even when an ordinary person (like me), or a bad person (like, say, Hitler), has a moment of openness, a moment of compassion, goodness rushes in to fill that space, to make us capable of receiving grace and transmitting it.

― Martha Beck, Expecting Adam: A True Story of Birth, Rebirth, and Everyday Magic."

About the Author

It is hard for cats to hold pens to write with and do not even get me started on the absurdity of using keyboards. I've even tried using the single claw method and it just proved to be excruciatingly slow.

So meet Sarah Saint-Laurent, a writer, Certified Martha Beck Life Coach, Energy Healer, and Mind Set Specialist. She is my best non-fur friend and when she is not busy working with clients developing the blueprint for their One True Life, she is kind enough to help me write my books.

Here's a little information about Sarah. Once, a former business executive, Sarah realized, like me, she wanted to live differently. Sarah now specializes in helping you learn to free yourself from things that no longer serve you. Whether you find yourself in the wrong relationship, marriage, job, dress size or other dead-end rut, Sarah will gently steer you on the path to clarity where you discover you have all of the answers, they are just hard to find under a pile of rubbish and fear-based thoughts. Using the techniques of visualization, Jungian-based dream analysis, spirit-guide journeying and deep listening combined with mindfulness teachings, deliberate creation, and body-centered techniques. If you are dealing with weight and body issues, Divorce, recovering from a relationship with a narcissist or other dark personality, Sarah has developed a program to return you to your rightful place, one of peace, clarity and empowerment.

You can check out her unique programs by requesting more information here:

http://wp.me/P5D95B-7J. Just insert into your browser

You can also explore Sarah's writings on major platforms like Elephant Journal here:

http://www.elephantjournal.com/2015/08/leaving-the-inner-mean-girls-club-confessions-of-a-recovering-approval-addict/

Made in the USA
Middletown, DE
27 July 2019